Iconic Rocks

Set II

Table of Contents

Written by Kassi Gilmour

Our land has many different landscapes, and some remarkable rocks have formed over time.

Many of our unusual rock landmarks have become icons and are well-known to people everywhere.

Wave Rock

Wave Rock is a well-known rock on the western side of our land. Looking like a massive wave, this perfectly curved granite rock attracts lots of travellers.

The Pinnacles

The Pinnacles are on the west coast. This landmark is the most popular park in WA. It is located north of Perth.

The Pinnacles are made up of thousands of tall rock pillars, made from limestone. They are scattered all over the yellow desert sands. Some have sharp, jagged sides and others are smooth.

Bungle Bungles

A fantastic assortment of beehive-shaped dome rocks can be seen in the north-west. These rocks are made from sandstone.

Bands of dark shades and rusty reds are easily seen in the layers of each dome rock.

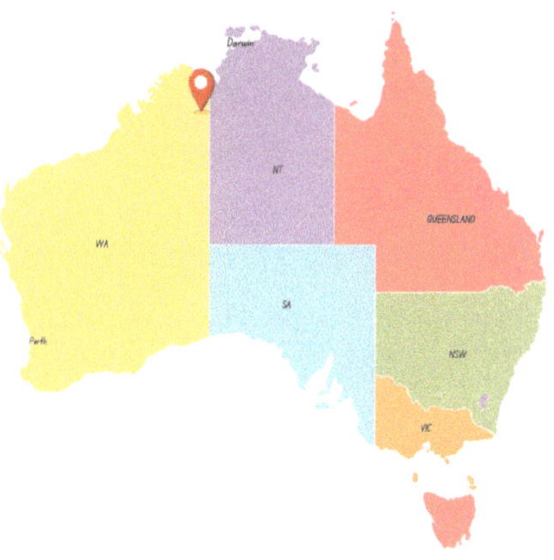

Nature's Window

Another popular spot on the west coast is Kalbarri. Rocky cliffs surround the winding river. Bands of rich reds, whites and darker shades of sandstone can be seen.

Nature's Window is an iconic lookout with an incredible outlook.

It is said that the ripples on the
rocks were formed by waves
and tides a long time ago.

Uluru

In the middle of our land stands our most iconic rock. Uluru is a massive rock made of red sandstone. It looks like it glows at sunrise and sunset.

Cascades, caves and rock art are all marvels at Uluru.

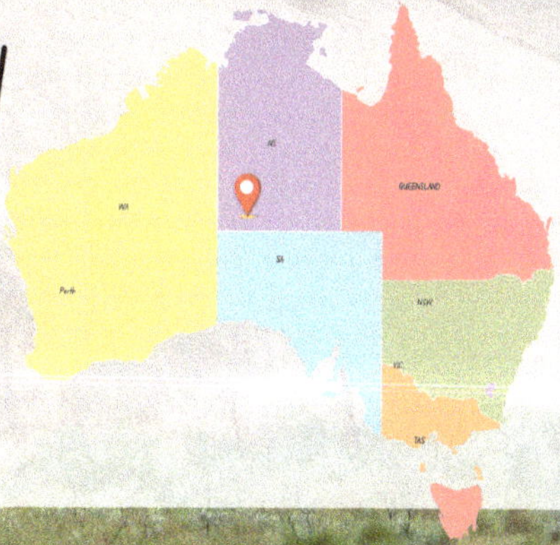

Three Sisters

On the eastern side of our land is the well-known Three Sisters. This landmark is located at Katoomba.

It is said that these rocks formed over a long time due to the eroding wind and rain.

The name of these rocks comes from a story about three sisters who turned to stone.

Tessellated Pavement

In Tasmania, there is a surprising pattern of rocks that looks like they have been tiled. This rock is mostly formed from *siltstone*.

Glass House Mountains

The remnants of an old volcano are a prominent landmark on the Sunshine Coast in Queensland. These rocky peaks were named by Captain James Cook when he sailed up the east coast.

The impressive *plugs* that stand tall today were formed when *molten* rock inside the volcano hardened.

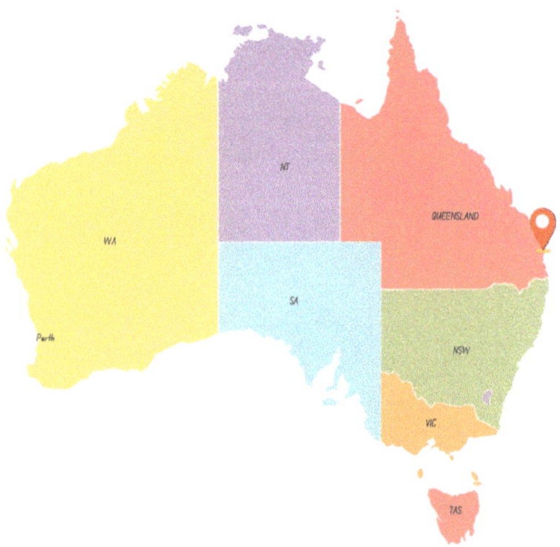

Glossary

dome - a rounded roof with a circular base.

eroding - gradually wear away by natural agents (wind, water).

granite - an igneous rock with great hardness.

icon - a symbol that is widely recognised and represents a place.

landmark - a feature that is easily seen and recognised.

limestone - a sedimentary rock made from calcium carbonate.

molten - melted into liquid by heat.

peaks - a mountain with a pointed summit.

pinnacle - a lofty peak.

plug - the inside part of a volcano after the lava hardens.

remnant - remaining pieces.

sandstone - sedimentary rock made with sand.

siltstone - a very fine-grained sandstone.

tessellated - a pattern of repeated shapes.

volcano - a vent in the earth where lava can be expelled.

Index

Vowels

The graphemes 'ur' and 'ir' represent the r-controlled vowel phoneme /er/, as in turn and girl.

The graphemes 'u_e' and 'ew' represent the long vowel phoneme /o͞o/, as in flute and drew.

These pictures help you remember the sound.